New Testament F
amongst
Dead Sea Scrolls

Bill Cooper

Copyright © Dr Wm R Cooper 2017

ISBN: 978-0-9931415-8-4

Published on Kindle under the title of

The Authenticity of the New Testament Fragments from Qumran.

This is for my daughters
Rebeccah and **Josephine**
mothers of the most
wonderful grandchildren
that a man was ever
blessed with.
Thank you both!

About the Author

Bill Cooper is a Vice President and Trustee of the Creation Science Movement in England. He also serves as Adjunct Professor of Providential History and Apologetics on the Master Faculty at the Institute for Creation Research School of Biblical Apologetics. He is the author of *After the Flood* (1995); *Paley's Watchmaker* (1997); *William Tyndale's 1526 New Testament* (old spelling ed. British Library. 2000); *The Wycliffe New Testament of 1388* (British Library. 2002); *The Authenticity of the Book of Genesis* (CSM. 2012); *The Authenticity of the Book of Daniel* (2012); *The Authenticity of the Book of Jonah* (2012); *The Authenticity of the Book of Esther* (2012); *The Chronicle of the Early Britons* (2012); *Old Light on the Roman Church* (2012); *The Authenticity of the New Testament Part 1: The Gospels* (2013); *The Authenticity of the New Testament Part 2: Acts, The Epistles and Revelation* (2013); *The Authenticity of the Book of Joshua* (2015); *The Authenticity of the Book of Judges* (2015). He has also authored numerous technical articles on Creationism, Palaeoanthropology, Bible Apologetics, the Reformation and the History of the English Bible. Graduating with Honours at Kingston University (England), he went on to obtain both his PhD and ThD from Emmanuel College of Christian Studies (Springdale, Arkansas). He lives in England, is married to Eileen (for more than 40 years now), has two daughters, numerous foster children, four grandsons and a granddaughter.

Acknowledgements

My heartiest thanks must go to Dr James J Scofield Johnson, Chief Academic Officer of the Institute for Creation Research School of Biblical Apologetics, my tutor and mentor in so many subjects. His expertise in Hebrew, Greek and Biblical Exegesis is invaluable, and is always freely at my disposal. My thanks also to Dr Gene Jeffries of Liberty University, whose past kindnesses, under the Lord, have made so much possible; to my good friend Dr Johnny Sanders of Downsville, Louisiana; to Leon Davey for his input; and last but by no means least, to Dr David and Joan Rosevear for their undying encouragement. Thank you all.

Cover illustration and Text composition

Text composition and cover design by L. Davey. The cover picture is of Qumran fragment 7Q4.1. It contains a portion of Paul's first letter to Timothy (1 Timothy 3:16-4:3).

Contents

Introduction

In 1955 there were discovered several papyrus fragments in Qumran Cave 7. The unusual – and unexpected – feature of Cave 7 was that all of its fragments were in Greek, as opposed to the exclusively Hebrew and Aramaic scrolls that had been found in the other caves. Apart from two of the fragments which were from the Greek version of the Old Testament (Exodus and the apocryphal Letter of Jeremiah), the rest of the fragments from Cave 7 were all catalogued as unidentified, and were considered indeed to be unidentifiable.

That's how things remained until 1972, when the papyrologist, Dr José O'Callaghan, thought that he would try to identify them. They were housed at the Rockefeller Museum in Jerusalem, and in April 1972 he was able to do a hands-on examination of each of them and to take a series of infra-red and other photographs. [1] What he discovered concerning them was to shock the academic world – the fragments belonged to books of the New Testament.

Why that should have shocked the world of academe was this. The cave and its fragments were sealed up in the year AD 68 when the Roman 10th Legion overran the area. This means that these New Testament books had been written out before that year, and were indeed copied out of earlier exemplars. It means that the New Testament had been written out and was in circulation well inside the Eyewitness Period of AD 30-70. In other words, it undermines everything - and I mean everything! - that the Bible critics have been saying for the past couple of hundred years or so. It means that the Gospels had not after all been a collection of oral traditions handed down over nigh a hundred years, growing all the while with the telling, as the critics have always claimed. It means that they were accounts that had been written out by eyewitnesses of Jesus' ministry, and even of His resurrection. They had heard His words and had written them down. It was just too much for the critics to swallow.

The howls of execration lasted for years. Nothing but ridicule and scorn was poured on O'Callaghan's head (it still is in fact), and he became the sniggeringstock of the academic world. The voices that supported him were very few indeed, and they soon found themselves drowned out by the din of protest. And yet O'Callaghan yielded not an inch. He knew the truth of what he had discovered, and issued numerous rebuttals of his critics (see Bibliography).

The main problem that the critics faced was that O'Callaghan knew more about his subject than they did, which is why he was able to rebut their every objection. So the critics did what they always do best. When your argument is weak, then shout longer and louder, and once your opponent can no longer be heard, then simply ignore him as if he had never been. It was a time-honoured strategy, and sometimes it worked. But not this time.

Here we will examine these fragments afresh, and we will consider all that O'Callaghan said about them. The critics have had their say. Since 1972, they have howled their protests and have cowed any and all who would dare to contradict them and their abysmally low view of the Scriptures. That will all come back to bite them one day. Meanwhile, we will consider the evidence which tells us so richly that our New Testament is no collection of fables written out so late that they are worthless, but a thoroughly authentic eyewitness account of the Man Christ Jesus, the Son of God. It is time for the fragments from Qumran Cave 7 to speak for themselves once again.

Bill Cooper

Footnotes to Introduction

1. O'Callaghan, 'The Identifications of 7Q', p. 287.

A Note on Textus Receptus and the Fragments of Cave 7

Textus Receptus, the Received Text, was long regarded among scholars – and rightly so - as the original Greek text of the New Testament. Afterwards exonerated by more than 5,000 early manuscript witnesses, it was published in print by Robert Stephens in 1550, and was the text from which all the Reformation Bibles of England and Europe up to the King James Bible were translated. Under the Hand of God, it went around the world, and is still loved and cherished by millions today.

Since the year 1881, however, Textus Receptus has faced a challenge – a serious worldwide effort to replace it with another text altogether, the Alexandrian or 'Critical' text. This 'Critical' text owes its origins to the Alexandrian Gnostics who, after the destruction of Jerusalem in AD 70, altered the text of the Scriptures to such a degree that hardly two of their texts ever agreed with each other. This seriously undermined the Authority of the Bible in the ancient world, just as it seriously undermines it today. It has been given its modern voice by all the discrepant versions that have been issued since the Revised Version of 1881, the brainchild of Westcott and Hort, and after them Nestle and Kurt Aland et al. In other words, confusion has reigned over what is the Word of God – if there truly is such a thing – and what are the later additions, amendments and omissions that have been made by those whose agenda has been to undermine that Word.

But herein lies the value of the New Testament fragments from Qumran Cave 7. They are all, without exception, from Textus Receptus. There is a very good reason for this. They were all sealed in Cave 7 by the year AD 68, that is two years before the destruction of Jerusalem and hence some years before the invention of the Alexandrian distortions of the Scriptures. In other words, the fragments represent the New Testament in its original state.

Ironically, O'Callaghan, who first identified the fragments as belonging to the New Testament, and Thiede who defended O'Callaghan's identifications throughout the 1990s and into the new millennium, used the Critical Text, as they called it, and not the Textus Receptus as the basis of their reconstructions. Perhaps they thought that scholars wouldn't listen to them if they used the Received Text. The irony here, however, is the fact that their identifications were entirely correct, although it did lead to one or two minor errors in the stichometry of their reconstructions. Where these occur, we have nitpickingly corrected them by supplying the stichometry from Textus Receptus, which is always an improvement in accuracy.

So, we have in the New Testament fragments from Cave 7, not only vital witnesses to the early writing and publication of the Books of the New Testament during the Eyewitness Period of AD 30-70, many decades before the critics would have us believe they were written, but witnesses also of the sheer antiquity and originality of the Received Text. It wasn't something dreamed up centuries later as Aland and colleagues have always taught, but was there at the beginning, written out during the Eyewitness Period, the very Words of God which inspired and were given to the New Testament writers. That is why these fragments are worth studying and preserving. They simply could not be more important.

Chapter One: 7Q4.1 & 7Q4.2 - 1 Timothy 3:16-4:3

The Discovery

When, in April 1972, Dr José O'Callaghan arrived in Jerusalem, he had no idea of the storm that was about to break over his head. He thought that he was going to the Rockefeller Museum in that city to try to identify the Old Testament books to which certain scraps of papyrus belonged. The scraps had been recovered in 1955 from Qumran Cave 7. There were nineteen of them altogether (one of which - 7Q19 - was actually an imprint in the floor of the cave of a papyrus that had dissolved away, leaving the ink behind to stain the soil), and two of them had already been identified ten years before as having belonged to the Book of Exodus and to an Old Testament apocryphal book called the Letter of Jeremiah. There was every expectation, therefore, that these remaining fragments would also be identified as belonging to certain Old Testament books, albeit they were all in Greek and not in Hebrew or Aramaic. All O'Callaghan had to do was to find out which ones they belonged to.

Their Greek raised no suspicions at all. It was assumed that the Greek Septuagint (LXX) version of the Old Testament would be the tree they fell out of. But he was soon to learn that that was not the case. The fragments could not be fitted into any Old Testament book at all, canonical or apocryphal, so O'Callaghan did the only thing he could think of. He tried to see if any of the books of the New Testament could accommodate them.

It was an unheard of procedure which went against the grain of everything that he'd been taught. The caves of Qumran, including Cave 7, had all been sealed shut in the year AD 68 to hide their contents from the Romans who were then flooding the area to hunt down Jewish rebels, and according to the critics, no New Testament books had been written out that early. What he found, therefore, came as a profound shock to him. No less than nine of the identifiable fragments could be shown to belong to no less than six New Testament books. It was impossible, but nonetheless true, and he now had a serious choice to make.

Dr O'Callaghan was an internationally esteemed member of academe. He was a leading papyrologist and founder of the Seminario de Papirología, and of the journal Studia Papirologica. Yet he knew that all he stood to gain from publishing his findings at the Rockefeller Museum would be ridicule from just about every branch of academe there is. That is a forbidding prospect for any man to face, and yet he was too honest to deny what he had discovered. His integrity would not allow that. So he took the bit between his teeth and he did publish what he found, and went on to defend what he found for many years to come against all kinds of assaults and challengers. But not once did he give in to them. In his mind there was absolutely no doubt about what he had discovered.

The immensity of his discovery's importance is too rarely appreciated, and these days it is even more rarely publicised. Only one champion of note ever laid his career and reputation on the line to defend O'Callaghan's work, and he is Dr Carsten Peter Thiede. The critics savaged him for doing it. In fact, they still savage him years after his untimely death.[1] Thiede was a world-class papyrologist who towered head and shoulders above his peers, and his defence of O'Callaghan's work was stoutly performed. We will be referring to much of Thiede's work as we progress, because he throws a great deal of light on areas which would otherwise go unnoticed.

In this present study, we will examine all the New Testament fragments from Cave 7, including the reverse-image imprint, 7Q19, that remained behind in the floor of the cave long enough to be photographed. This is the first occasion in a good many years on which the fragments have been examined in depth together in the same volume - in fact, it comes as a surprise that no one has ever dealt with all the fragments from Cave 7 before, not even O'Callaghan. Starting with the first in numerical order, we will begin with 7Q4.1 & 7Q4.2, in which are preserved a portion of Paul's First Letter to Timothy - 1 Timothy 3:16-4:3.

7Q4.1 & 7Q4.2 - 1 Timothy 3:16-4:3

Fig.1: 7Q4.1   Fig.2: 7Q4.2

7Q4 is a papyrologist's delight. Usually, fragments of texts on papyrus come from the middle of a page, a paragraph, or a line, and then the one deciphering its contents has a lot of work to do. How many letters were there to a line, what letters were they, and how many lines were there to a page? While he is occupied with that, he has to work out, if he can, what literary work the text is a fragment of. He has to make a note of all the surviving letters that can be discerned, and then try to reconstruct all the letters of which only parts or traces remain. To do this, he has to be something of an expert in the language and even dialect that the text is written in, as well as all the nuances and foibles of its calligraphy, and so on. In short, it can be a mammoth task just trying to offer a reconstruction that makes any sense. He knows that waiting in the wings are a whole tribe of scholars whose only interest in life seems to be to question and preferably undo all the work he has done, and hopefully ruin his reputation as a scholar while they're at it. The scholars of academe can be vicious when they want to be. They will pounce on any uncertainty as a disproof and will milk that for all it is worth, even long after their objections have been answered. They have to. There is a great deal at stake, and it's a lot more than just their own reputations and professorial chairs.

That is why 7Q4 is such a satisfying find. It doesn't come from the middle of a page. It comes from the outside edge, the very end of the scroll, preserving beautifully the last words of each line. That makes the papyrologist's work so much more straightforward. The stichometry (line and letter-count) that he has to work out is simplified immensely, because he knows exactly where each line terminates. That is an enormous plus.

In Figures 1 & 2 above, we can see the fragment almost exactly as it was found. Figure 2 constitutes the last line of text (Line 9), but there was another tiny scrap, now lost by all accounts, which constituted Line 8 of the fragment and which contained two letters,]??[. When these fragments were first published in 1962 in what came to be known as the editio princeps of the Cave 7 fragments, not one of them was identified as belonging to the New Testament, and this particular tiny scrap was transcribed by the editors with simply two dots]..[, indicating that its letters were unidentifiable.[2] O'Callaghan identified them both though.

Here is O'Callaghan's initial transcription of 7Q4's surviving letters (given in Greek cursive rather than the uncial or capital letters of the fragment):

1.   ]η
2.   ]των
3.   ]ονται
4.   ]πνευ
5.   ]ημο
6.   [ ]
7.   [ ]
8.   ]ντ[
9.   ]Οθε[

... and here is his reconstruction of the fragment's stichometry, showing how the letters are remnants of Paul's first letter to Timothy:[3]

1.   [σινεπιστευθηενκοσμωανελημφθ]**η**.............28 letters
2.   [ενδοξη   τοδεπνευμαρε]**των**............21 letters (with 7 letter gap)
3.   [λεγιυστεροισκαιροισαποστησ]**ονται**..........31 letters
4.   [τινεστησπιστεωσπροσεχοντεσ]**πνευ**............30 letters
5.   [μασινπλανησκαιδιδασκαλιαισδ]**ημο**...........30 letters[4]
6.   [νιωνενυποκρισειψευδολογωνκε].................27 letters
7.   [καυστηριασμενωντηνιδιανσουνει]..............28 letters
8.   [δησινκωλιο]**ντ**[ωνγαμεινσπεχεσθαι]...........29 letters[5]
9.   [βρωματωνα]**οθε**[οσεκτισενεισμετα]...........28 letters

There was only one brave attempt of any note to disprove the Pauline provenance of 7Q4, and that was collectively made by Nebe, Muro and Puech, each of whom tried to show that it was in fact from the apocryphal Book of

Enoch.[6] They all failed, and they failed dismally, mainly because they had to stretch the stichometry of the fragment to breaking point, and had to invent oddities of grammar and vocabulary entirely unknown in ancient Greek literature. Thiede explains how they went astray textually,[7] but we show how they went astray in a more amusing way in Chapter Nine below.

Footnotes to Chapter One

1. I had the honour and privilege of talking with Dr Thiede on two occasions; once at a Tyndale Society Conference at Hertford College, Oxford, and later at Lambeth Palace shortly before he tragically died of a heart attack at his home in Paderborn, Germany, aged just 52. Bible apologetics lost one of its most able champions that day.

2. Baillet, M, Milik J, & Vaux R (eds.). 'Les Petites Grottes de Qumran.' Discoveries in the Judaean Desert. Vol. 3. (issued in 2 vols: Textes et Planches). 1962. Clarendon Press, Oxford.

3. O'Callaghan, Los Papiros Griegos de Cueva 7 de Qumran, p. 42.

4. Both O'Callaghan (Los Papiros Griegos de la Cueva 7 de Qumran. p. 42), and Thiede, (Dead Sea Scrolls, p. 157), give a letter-count for line 5 of 31 letters. It seems they had forgotten that Baillet's 1962 editio princeps of the fragment, which gave ???? for the line's surviving letters, had already been corrected by O'Callaghan to ???, which reduces the line to one of 30 letters.

5. It seems that the tiny scrap remaining of line 8 was either lost or deteriorated to nothing sometime after O'Callaghan's examination of the Q7 fragments at Jerusalem.

6. Nebe, G. '7Q4 - Möglichkeit und Grenze einer Identifikation.' Revue de Qumran. vol. 13 (1988). pp. 629-633.

7. Thiede, The Earliest Gospel Manuscript? pp. 50-52.

Chapter Two: 7Q5 - Mark 6:52-53

Fig. 3: Fragment 7Q5 of Mark 6:52-53

There arose a mighty hoo-ha when O'Callaghan identified 7Q5 as being a portion of Mark 6:52-53. The critics were not kind. 'There is not enough of it to allow such an identification,' it was objected. 'It has only 20 letters or parts of letters on only 5 lines of text. It is therefore not possible to make any identification. It could be anything. It is not enough!'... and so on.

It is wondrous strange then that these same scholars were ready enough to accept 7Q2 as a portion of Baruch 6 – the Letter of Jeremiah, found in the same cave as 7Q5. For that fragment has 22 letters on also only five lines of text, just two letters more than 7Q5 has. Moreover, five of its 22 letters are indistinct, and the two words only that can be made out, ουν and αυτος, are too common to be distinctive. Furthermore, when Benoit and Boismard made the identification, they could do so only "by presupposing textual variants much more difficult than those found in 7Q5."[1] Yet few have ever challenged *that* identification.

So, what is the difference between the two fragments, 7Q2 and 7Q5? The answer is simple. Baruch 6 (the Letter of Jeremiah) is part of the Old Testament Apocrypha – not a Biblical book, but an add-on by those who would add to God's Word. The presence of such a writing as early as AD 68 would not be a surprise, and would therefore not rock the Bible critic's boat. But a book from the New Testament at such a date? Such a suggestion is rank heresy to the critics, and hence the thunder which is still rumbling today.

However, when it comes to identifying fragments such as these, the papyrologist is constrained to looking at probabilities, and it cannot be insignificant that the mathematician, Albert Dou (1915-2009), has calculated that the chances of the fragment 7Q5 *not* being that of Mark 6:52-53 is less than 1 in 900,000,000,000.[2] That is an impressive probability indeed. Under the terms and parameters of Probability Theory that makes it a certainty, and it is possible only for the singular fact that no other text exists which 7Q5 could belong to. The critics can huff and puff as much as they like, it is a fact. There is no other. This much was proven by the independent Ibycus computer analysis of the fragment. The programme contained every extant Greek text there is, and the only match that it found was Mark 6:52-53, which was O'Callaghan's identification exactly.[3]

Furthermore, and quite separate from the computer analysis, the fragment was subjected to a forensic examination at the Israel National Police Forensic Laboratory in Jerusalem.[4] Now it cannot be imagined that the Israeli Police Force have any historical interest at all in vindicating the New Testament. Yet their investigation only confirmed the identification, and in fact increased its certainty, for it prevented a possible misreading of at least one of the partial letters.[5]

O'Callaghan gives a full explanation of the fragment in his 1974 monograph.[6] However, his original hands-on examination of the Cave 7 papyri at Jerusalem over a two-week period is invariably ignored by his critics:

"... Aland has chosen not to include my identifications, not even that of 7Q5, in the list of NT papyri, because, he says, I have worked only with photographs. Aland insists on this position and never mentions my examination of the papyri of 7Q in the Rockefeller Museum in Jerusalem, where I worked for two weeks in late April, 1972. Even though he should be aware of this, Aland ignores it, as he does my general ratification of the readings previously verified in the same museum."[7]

Aland knew perfectly well that O'Callaghan had examined the papyri at firsthand, because he cites O'Callaghan's paper in which that examination is described in full.[8] It is worth noting here, though, that in fact it was Aland himself who had never set eyes on the 7Q fragments. Between himself and O'Callaghan, he was the only one to have worked only from photographs. Whether the crass hypocrisy of his position ever dawned on him we shall never know. But if he was happy to lie about and defame O'Callaghan, then it probably wouldn't have bothered him. Aland was the leading critic of his day, and his anti-Biblical ambitions were revealed when he called for the New Testament's Pastoral Epistles to be dropped from the Scriptural Canon.[9] In fact, he believed *all* of the New Testament Books to be spurious. Such a man is no fit judge of archaeological evidence that vindicates the New Testament, yet for many years he was the critics' 'gatekeeper' who got to say which evidence would be accepted – taught in our universities and released to the public - and which would remain hidden. He was hardly going to allow evidence through which entirely contradicted all that he had ever said on the matter.

Aland had, it is true, subjected the text of 7Q5 to a computer analysis at his institute at Münster, in Germany, but even this was heavily loaded to find against O'Callaghan's identification of 7Q5:

"... the most influential voice against it, that of K. Aland, has sounded convincing to many of his readers for an apparently valid reason: Aland used the computer at his institute in Münster in order to analyse two different combinations of letters which he thought were possible 'minimal' readings of the fragment 7Q5.... But as Rohrhirsch shows, Aland's efforts *had* to fail for a methodological reason, not because of any shortcomings of the fragment itself. The obvious – but unrecognised reason (neither O'Callaghan nor I had seen this particular mistake of Aland's before Rohrhirsch's publication): no existing edition of the Greek text of Mark has the variant *tau* for *delta* in the [word on line 3 of the fragment] 'diaperasantes'. Thus, Aland's computer programme of the Greek New Testament, based here on the *delta*, had to miss Mark 6:52-53 as a possible passage, and it promptly did."[10]

To his everlasting credit, O'Callaghan ploughed on, regardless of the critics, patiently publishing numerous rebuttals to their objections; all of which helped immensely, for it gave O'Callaghan (as well as ourselves) the opportunity to fine-tune the arguments. And it is worth noting that all this fine-tuning led to not one of his identifications being changed. They were certainly challenged (though not all), but none were ever changed. They were only strengthened by the process. The papyrus evidence from Cave 7 is that good. But now let's look at the fragment itself.

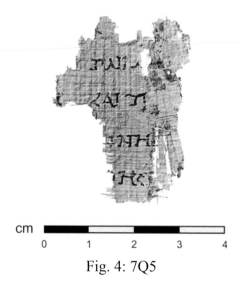

cm
0   1   2   3   4

Fig. 4: 7Q5

Fragment 7Q5 contains, as noted, 20 letters (whole, partial and traces) on five lines of text (what was the top line is practically obliterated with just a trace of the letter ε visible) – see Fig. 4 above. The characters are written on the papyrus in uncials (what we would call capital letters -]E[ ]YTΩNH[ ]H KAIT[ ]NNHΣ[ ]ΘHΣA[-) and without spaces, (the large three-letter space or 'spatium' in Line 4 between H   KAIT being a paragraphus, is exactly what is expected at this place in Mark's Gospel). But for some mysterious reason, scholars commonly insist on copying out the letters in miniscule (lower case). So here are the surviving letters of 7Q5, in Greek miniscule, after O'Callaghan:

1.   ]ε[
2.   ]υτωνη[
3.   ]η.....καιτ[
4.   ]ννησ[
5.   ]Θησα[

According to O'Callaghan, the way they fit into the verses of Mark 6:52-53 is like this:

1.   συνηκαν]ε[πιτοισαρτοισ...............................20 letters
2.   αλληνα]υτωνη[καρδιαπεπωρω......................23 letters
3.   μεν]η.....καιτι[απερασαντεσ...........................20 letters (inc. the 'spatium')
4.   ηλθονεισΓε]ννησ[αρετκαι...........................21 letters
5.   προσωρμισ]θησα[νκαιεξελ...........................21 letters[11]

This reading by O'Callaghan is based on an estimated stichometry (letter-count) of an average 21 letters to a line. That's fine, except that the proposed stichometry must omit three words that are included in the Gospel of Mark. Those words are επι την γην, and they mean 'into the land of'. They should have appeared on line 4 above, just before the word Γεννησαρετ (Gennesaret). So instead of reading, "they came into the land of Gennesaret," (Textus Receptus), the fragment would read (with this stichometry), "they landed at Gennesaret."

The meaning of the sentence is not affected by the omission, and O'Callaghan points out, citing Legg, that this same omission is not unknown in other early manuscripts of Mark.[12] But Legg was publishing a volume of the Westcott and Hort Greek New Testament which does omit the words επι την γην, and he was naturally looking for texts that deviated from the Textus Receptus.[12] That is because Westcott and Hort relied on the Alexandrian text, and the Alexandrian Gnostics didn't begin tampering with and perverting the original New Testament (Textus Receptus) until some considerable time after the year AD 68 when this fragment of Mark (7Q5) was sealed up at Qumran. Therefore 7Q5 could not be a representative of the Alexandrian. Ironically, the main Alexandrian text on which Westcott and Hort famously relied was Codex Sinaiticus, and that *does* include επι την γην.[13]

The omission – assuming O'Callaghan's estimated stichometry to be accurate – must therefore be a simple scribal omission. The omission could easily have been supplied in the marginalia or between the lines above where the words επι την γην should have appeared. After all, that was the common way of supplying omissions back then, and we cannot exclude that probability just because the fragment, being a mere fragment, cannot show such an apparatus in play. But it is legitimate to make the assumption, just as it is legitimate to assume a stichometry of an average 21 letters to a line.

There is another stick with which the critics commonly beat this fragment, and that is the 'unorthodox' spelling of the word on Line 3: τι[απερασαντεσ] – ti[aperasantes] – which means "having crossed over". Instead of beginning with a τ (tau), it was usually spelt with a δ (delta) and as far as the critics are concerned, this disproves the fact that 7Q5 is from Mark's Gospel. However, if only our critics would take the bother to look around them and examine some inscriptions of the time, they would find the same dialectical substitution of tau for delta in an official inscription; and not just any old official inscription, but one which once adorned the Temple in Jerusalem. The notice forbad any Gentile to enter the Temple court on pain of death, and instead of the word for barrier, δρυφακτος, being given its common spelling, it is spelt τρυφακτος, its initial letter delta being replaced by tau, just as in 7Q5.[14]

The substitution is down purely to a Judaean dialect of the Greek language, a simple matter of the preferred pronunciation of a hard τ rather than a soft δ, and the example above is not alone in attesting to that fact.[15] If anything, the substitution is one of the evidences which proclaim the fragment's authenticity, because a forger (or a dull-witted O'Callaghan) would never have thought of it. Thiede goes on to inform us that in a text dated to AD 42, τικες is given for δικες. Moreover, "Numerous Biblical papyri have the δ to τ shift."[16] In other words, the apparent misspelling of διαπερασαντες in 7Q5 isn't a misspelling at all, but a common enough occurrence for the authenticity of 7Q5's identification as Mark 6:52-53 not to be called into question by it. The critics are not ignorant of these facts. They know them well enough. But the fact that they ignore them speaks volumes both for the fatuousness of their own position and the true identity of 7Q5 as Mark 6:52-53.

The critics, of course, do not stop there. They contest the ν (N = nu) on line 2 of the fragment, because it is only partially represented. It is not a nu at all, they say, thinking that no nus must be good nus. But microscopic infrared analysis, stereo-microscopy, simple stichometry and the evidence of one's own eyes, tell a different story. It certainly is the letter *v*, giving the reading of line 2 the letters υτωνη.[17] That's exactly what they should be for Mark's Gospel.

Meanwhile, the reader is directed toward Appendix One of this present study for a translation of the Israeli Police forensic report into the fragment, where the fragment was subjected to the most searching analysis. Had there been the slightest indication that 7Q5 was not from Mark's Gospel, it would have shown up under *this* investigation if under no other. But not the slightest indication was given. The fragment is 100% from Mark's Gospel, and we know by that fact that Mark's Gospel was written out and in circulation well before the year AD 68.[18] Are the critics happy with that fact? No. No, they're not. That's why they either ignore it or do their best to shout it down.

Footnotes to Chapter Two

1. As noted by Thiede, *The Earliest Gospel Manuscript? p.* 42. The position for 7Q2 was actually worse than Thiede states. Randall Price tells us: "The identification of 7Q2 with Baruch/*Letter of Jeremiah* 6:43-44 (which is undisputed) faced even greater textual difficulties, having only *one* clearly discernible letter." *Secrets of the Dead Sea Scrolls*, p. 185.

2. Dou, Albert, 'El calculo des probabilidades y las posibles identificaciones de 7Q5', pp. 116-139 of O'Callaghan's *Los Primeros Testimonios del Nuevo Testamento*, Madrid, 1995.

3. Thiede, Carsten Peter. 'Greek Qumran Fragment 7Q5: Possibilities and Impossibilities.' *Biblica.* Vol. 75. No. 3 (1994), p. 395. The Ibycus computer's search engine was *Thesaurus Linguae Graecae, which was able to scan more than 64,000,000 words in extant Greek works ranging from those of Homer, all the way up to AD 1453 (the year Constantinople fell to Turkish invaders). Which makes the* objection raised by the critics that this computer analysis cannot be accepted because it didn't take into account all those Greek texts that are no longer extant, one of the silliest things I've ever read. Incredibly, this was and still is put forward for serious consumption. I sigh, but only because it is less effort to sigh than to laugh.

4. For a detailed discussion, see Thiede's, 'Bericht über die kriminaltechnische Untersuchung des Fragments 7Q5 in Jerusalem.' [Report on the forensic examination of the fragment 7Q5 in Jerusalem]. *Christen und Christliche.* 1992. Friedrich Pustet. Regensburg. pp. 239-245. The article is in German, but see my translation in Appendix One below.

5. Ibid.

6. O'Callaghan, José. *Los Papiros Griegos de la Cueva 7 de Qumran.* 1974. pp. 44-61.

7. O'Callaghan, 'The Identifications of 7Q', p. 287.

8. 'Notas sobre 7Q tomadas en el Rockefeller Museum de Jerusalén.' *Biblica.* 53 (1972), pp. 517-533. Cited by Aland in his 'Neue neutestamentliche Papyri III.' *New Testament Studies.* Vol. 20 (1974). pp. 357-376.

9. See Aland's: *The problem of Anonymity and Pseudonymity in Christian Literature of the First Two Centuries* (1961); & *The Problem of the New*

Testament Canon (1962). Aland dedicated his entire life to the undermining, dishonouring and defaming of the Scriptures. He died in 1994.

10. Thiede, *The Earliest Gospel Manuscript? p.* 40. n. 31.

11. *Los Papiros Griegos de la Cueva 7 de Qumran.* p. 59.

12. *Los Papiros Griegos de la Cueva 7 de Qumran*, p. 60. The work cited by O'Callaghan here is: Legg, S C E. *Nouum Testamentum Graece Secundum Textum Westcotto-Hortianum Euangelium Sedundum Marcum.* 1935. Clarendon Press. Oxonii. The volume is unpaginated, but the cited entry appears in the *apparatus criticus*.

13. Codex Sinaiticus Q76:6r. But see Cooper, *The Forging of Codex Sinaiticus.* 2016. CSM & Kindle.

14. Thiede, *Dead Sea Scrolls*, pp. 176-177. Likewise, O'Callaghan points this out: "Mas aun, en Jerusalen encontramos testimoniada dicha anomalia fonetica. Se trata nada menos que de una inscripcion hallada en el templo de Herodes. En ella leemos ΤΡΥΦΑΚΤΟΥ en vez de ΔΡΥΦΑΚΤΟΥ. No creo necesario insistir mas en la prodigalidad de dicho cambio." *Los Papiros Griegos de la Cueva 7 de Qumran.* p. 53.

15. See Liddell and Scott's *Greek-English Lexicon.*

16. Thiede, *Dead Sea Scrolls*, p. 244, citing: Cignac's, *Grammar of the Greek Papyri of the Roman and Byzantine Periods, 1. Phonology.* 1976. Milan. pp. 80-83. O'Callaghan also says something on the subject in his, 'El cambio δ>τ en P. Chester Beatty XIII.' *Biblica.* 60 (1979), pp. 415-416.

17. Thiede, *The Earliest Gospel Manuscript?* pp. 35-38.

18. For more evidence of Mark's early writing, and especially the impact that his Gospel had on contemporary Roman literature, see Cooper, *The Authenticity of the New Testament part 1: The Gospels*, Chapter Six, and Appendix Two.

Chapter Three: 7Q6.1 – Mark 4:28

Fig. 5: 7Q6.1

Surprisingly, this fragment, being also from the Gospel of Mark, does not belong to the same scroll as 7Q5. Its handwriting is quite different. 7Q5 bears a type of calligraphy known as Herodian "Zierstil," meaning a decorated style with short hooks and strokes, or flourishes, which one particular school of calligraphy preferred, and as O'Callaghan tells us:

"... we note that this papyrus [7Q6.1] does not belong to "Zierstil," but to a different palaeographic school, which in this case seems to be [similar] to [that of] Herculaneum."[1] (My translation)

That is very interesting. Herculaneum (which in AD 68 was still a flourishing city of great wealth and culture) stands on the west coast of Italy, a little south of Naples, and Thiede argues a very strong case for the fact that the Cave 7 documents were written out at Rome and exported from there to Qumran.[2] What more natural, then, if several scribes are involved in the copying, by dictation no doubt, that they will write in different styles of Italian/Greek calligraphy? One will write in the 'Zierstil' style in which he has been trained, whilst another sitting next to him, having come from Herculaneum and trained in that style, will use that favoured by the Herculaneum school. But the fact that there are four fragments of Mark – 7Q5; 7Q6.1; 7Q7; & 7Q15 – which are written in *four* different hands but on the same papyrus batch, suggests not only that serious efforts were being made to copy and distribute books of the New Testament – particularly the Gospel of Mark - very early on, but that the papyri of Cave 7 represent a collection of New Testament documents, some of which were multiple copies of the same books – a veritable bookstore certainly, but also probably a Christian reference or lending library. This suggestion of such a working library will be greatly enhanced when we come to examine 7Q19 in Chapter Twelve below. But whilst that will excite the Christian believer, the notion is not welcomed by everyone.

The very fact that there were at least four copies of Mark found in Q7 extracted from Kurt Aland his famously explosive dismissal: *"Das sprengt doch wohl alle Möglichkeiten der Phantasie!"* - "This exceeds all possible bounds of fantasy!"[3] But then, how would he know? Aland was the leading 'Higher Critic' of his day who despised the New Testament and all who would defend it, and he treated with equal disdain any supporting evidence that was invoked in its defence. Was he a papyrologist? No, he wasn't. Papyrology is a science, whereas higher criticism – so called – is a highly negative anti-Biblical philosophy which is based on nothing more than conjecture, whim, wordplay and prejudice. To put it bluntly, it is anti-knowledge, nothing more, and Aland was a past master at it.

However, we know that 7Q6.1 belongs to Mark (4:28) because of the letters that are preserved on the fragment and their stichometry. When the two are combined, calligraphy and stichometry together, they form a match that is found in no other document, so the identification is very certain. When first the fragment was published by Baillet in 1962, he and his colleagues showed a not-too-surprising reticence in identifying its letters. We needn't ask why. Like Aland, they also were leading higher critics, and if any of the editors and authors of that volume had dared to suggest that they were dealing with New Testament documents here, their careers and reputations would have ended abruptly.

O'Callaghan showed no such reticence, of course. He was a papyrologist, not a critic, and his initial reading (aided by a hands-on microscopic examination along with infra-red and other photographs of 7Q6.1) is as follows:

1.   ]φ[
2.   ]ειτεν[
3.   ]πληρη[^{4}

Estimating a stichometry of an average 18 letters to a line, O'Callaghan shows how these fit into the verse, Mark 4:28, as follows:

1.   [ηγηκαρπο]φ[ορειπρωτον]..............19 letters
2.   [χορτον]ειτεν[σταχυν].....................17 letters
3.   [ειτεν]πληρη[σιτονεντω].................19 letters^5

There is absolutely no document on this good earth of ours to which this fragment can belong other than Mark's Gospel, in particular its 4th chapter and 28th verse. So Aland and his colleagues can explode as much as they like. After 60 years and more of effort and ingenuity, not one of them can show what other document this fragment can be from. There is no other, and we can only wonder at the abhorrence among them that this invokes. One thing is made very clear by it, though, and that is the fact that in spite of their claim to be impartial and honest enquirers, our Bible critics are nothing of the kind. Aland's reaction was pure and very hostile emotion, and it is an all too common reaction amongst his colleagues when confronted with evidence of this kind.

The early, even contemporaneous copying and distribution of New Testament documents, Gospels and Letters, seems to be obliquely referred to by the apostle Paul, when he asks:

"And when this epistle is read among you, cause that it be read also in the church of the Laodiceans; and that ye likewise read the epistle from Laodicea."^{6}

It would be hard for his readers to do this if these epistles were not copied and available for other congregations to study, and it is easy to see how New Testament libraries would very soon spring up all over the Roman Empire. The collection recovered from Qumran Cave 7 should therefore be seen as the glorious rule rather than as the exception.[7]

Footnotes to Chapter Three

1. O'Callaghan, Los Papiros Griegos de la Cueva 7 de Qumran, p. 62: "... notamos que este papiro no pertenece al "Zierstil," sino a una escuela paleografica distinta, que en este caso parece ser la de Herculano."

2. Thiede, Dead Sea Scrolls, pp. 95-97. See also his, The Earliest Gospel Manuscript? pp. 53-54. Elsewhere, in his 'Papyrus Magdalen Greek 17 (Gregory-Aland64) A Reappraisal.' Zeitschrift für Papyrologie und Epigraphik, Bd. 105 (1995), p. 17, Thiede brings out the point that Herculaneum was destroyed in the Vesuvius eruption of AD 79. This means that the Herculaneum style of calligraphy would have come to end around that time, so any document bearing its characteristic style of writing would have to have been written out before that date. In other words, it is a style of calligraphy that we would expect to find on a document that had been written in or before AD 68.

3. Aland, 'Neue Neutestamentliche Papyri III.' New Testament Studies. Vol. 20 (1974). pp. 362-363.

4. Los Papiros Griegos de la Cueva 7 de Qumran, p. 64.

5. Ibid.

6. Colossians 4:16. The letter of Paul to the Laodiceans was never included in the New Testament Canon, but it has survived in a fragmentary Latin translation preserved in ancient copies of Jerome's Latin Vulgate Bible and in some copies of the Wycliffe Bible. For a full discussion of Laodiceans, see Cooper, 'Part 2: Paul's 'Lost Letter to the Laodicean Church,' Old Light on the Roman Church (Kindle).

7. For more on the copying and publishing of the New Testament during the Eyewitness Period (AD 30-70), see Cooper, The Authenticity of the New Testament, Part One: The Gospels, Chapter Three.

Chapter Four: 7Q6.2 – Acts 27:38

Fig. 6: 7Q6.2

This fragment's catalogue number was given as 7Q6.2 because it was assumed that it had belonged to 7Q6.1 on which it was resting when found.[1] But in fact it belongs to a different Book of the New Testament altogether, namely the Book of Acts (27:38).

At the time this fragment was written out, the Book of Acts was surprisingly new. It is estimated that Luke wrote Acts in AD 66, which means that this copy of Acts was made within only a year of the original's completion. That is hugely embarrassing for the critics. The Westar Institute, for instance, home to the infamous Jesus Seminar, recently published the findings of their Acts Seminar, findings which they took ten years to reach, and which sought to show that Acts was written out by an impostor passing himself off as Luke, a good hundred years or more after the real Luke – if there ever was such a person – had died.[2] However, the level of scholarship employed by the Institute to reach their findings was abysmally poor – derelict in fact - and I have answered their claim elsewhere.[3] Suffice it here to say that the solitary and single fact of Luke's Acts being discovered amongst other New Testament Books in a cave that was sealed up in AD 68, is alone sufficient to demolish their nonsense. That is the value of the Qumran Cave 7 fragments. There is simply no arguing with them.

As for 7Q6.2 itself, it was written in the "Zierstil" style, unlike 7Q6.1 with which it was at first associated by Baillet *et al*, which was written in the Herculaneum style.[4] O'Callaghan identified the surviving letters as:

1.   ]Κορ[
2.   ]ουφι[[5]

.... and supplying a stichometry of 22/23 letters per line, he shows how it is most certainly identified with Acts 27:38, and with Acts 27:38 alone:

1.   [δομηκονταεξ]**κορ**[εσθεντεσ]........22 letters
2.   [δετροφησεκ]**ουφι**[ζοντοπλοι].......23 letters[6]

But there is yet another most important point of interest here which makes the identification of 7Q6.2 with Acts 27:38 even more certain, and that is the fact that the fragment contains on Line 2 components of the word 'εκουφιζον' which appears only once in the New Testament, and in this precise form not once in all extant Greek literature:[7]

"And when they had eaten enough, they *lightened* [εκουφιζον] the ship, and cast out the wheat into the sea." Acts 27:38

The Greek term for this kind of word is *hapax legomenon* – 'απαξ λεγομενον - a thing said only once. Because they are unique, such *hapax legomena* are most important when it comes to identifying such fragments, and it is nothing less than Providential that the fragment 7Q6.2 has preserved this particular example. It explains why the critics have never seriously challenged 7Q6.2. They have offered some very strained suggestions for identifying some of the other Q7 fragments as representing other than New Testament texts, not one of which has succeeded except to embarrass the proposer, but they have always steered well clear of this one. 'Εκουφιζον' appears in no other Greek text known to man. Simply put, it is unique to Acts 27:38.

Now that leaves the critics with a very serious problem, because 7Q6.2's certain identification as a New Testament text, one that is found in Qumran Cave 7, very much enforces the probability of other less certain and more damaged fragments from Q7 also belonging to New Testament texts. Along with other fragments, it shows the certain presence of the Christian Scriptures at Qumran at a time when – according to the critics - they should not even have existed, and so they testify against everything that the critics have always claimed. According to the critics, nothing but Old Testament and related texts are to be found at Qumran, and the admission that Christian texts are also to be found there would mean the rewriting of whole libraries and the loss of the many reputations of those who wrote them. But there it is. Facts are facts are facts.

Footnotes to Chapter Four

1. O'Callaghan, *Los Papiros Griegos de la Cueva 7 de Qumran.* 1974. 61. – "Papiro fino, en muy mal estado. Los dos fragmentos se encontraron adheridos uno sobre el otro. Por haber sido deteriorados conjuntamente, tienen contornos en parte parecidos." – "Fine papyrus, in very bad condition. The two fragments [7Q6.1 & 7Q6.2] were found stuck together. Having been damaged together, they have similar contours." (my translation)

2. Smith, D & Tyson J (eds.). *Acts and Christian Beginnings: The Acts Seminar Report.* 2013. Polebridge Press. (Westar Institute).

3. See Cooper, *The Authenticity of the New Testament, Part 2: Acts, the Epistles, and Revelation,* chapters one and two.

4. O'Callaghan, *Los Papiros Griegos de la Cueva 7 de Qumran.* 1974. p. 66. – "La escritura de este papiro pertenece tambien al "Zierstil" (adviertase la perfeccion en el trazado de la φ) y puede datarse, al igual que 7Q5, como de la mitad del siglo 1." – "The writing of this papyrus also belongs to "Zierstil" (note the perfection in drawing φ) and can be dated, like 7Q5, to the middle of the 1st century." (my translation)

5. Ibid.

6. Ibid.

7. Ibid., pp. 65-66. See also Liddell & Scott's, *Greek-English Lexicon,* pp. 837-838.

Chapter Five: 7Q7 – Mark 12:17

Fig. 7: 7Q7

If we gave this fragment nothing more than a mere cursory glance, it wouldn't strike us as very promising. Yet even here we may identify 7Q7 as the fragment of a New Testament text. Using O'Callaghan's reconstruction of a stichometry around the surviving letters, (which he gives as):

1. [....]
2.]ο[
3.]και[
4.]θαυ[¹

.... we may see that the fragment is, in fact, part of Mark 12:17 – "And Jesus answering said unto them, Render to Caesar the things that are Caesar's, and to God the things that are God's. And they marvelled at him." – which in the 'Critical' text used by O'Callaghan reads thus:

"... Καισαρος. ¹⁷ο δε Ιησους ειπεν αυτοις Τα Καισαρος αποδοτε Καισαρι, τα του θεου τω θεω. Και εξεθαυμαζον επ αυτω. ¹⁸Και...."²

Taking even this text, O'Callaghan was able to show that, with a stichometry averaging 21 letters to a line, Mark 12:17 would have appeared on 7Q7 written thus:

1. [καισαροσ........οδεισειπεν].............18 letters
2. αυτ]ο[ιστακαισαροσαποδο]..............21 letters
3. τε]και[σαριτατουθυτωθωκαιε].........24 letters
4. ξε]θαυ[μαζονεπαυτωκαιερ]...............21 letters³

From this we see that O'Callaghan's proposed stichometry gives an exact match for Mark 12:17. You will have noticed, however, that the verse, when written conventionally, contains seven letters more than does the stichometry. This is due to the use in early papyri of what is known in palaeography as *nomina sacra* – sacred names – which are reduced thus: Instead of writing the name of Jesus in full, i.e. Ιησους, early copyists would often employ the contraction Ις; and for God, i.e. θεος, they would employ θς, marking each occurrence above with a short straight line called a macron to show that this is a sacred name - *nomen sacrum*. But what is important here is this. The use of such contractions when writing sacred names was an exclusively Christian usage, and the stichometry employed here shows such contractions to have been used in the document known to us as 7Q7.

However, and I hate to say this, but O'Callaghan used the wrong text for Mark 12:17 in his reconstruction of the fragment's stichometry.⁴ He was right to identify the fragment as Mark 12:17, but he used the Westcott and Hort text, known popularly as the 'critical text,' for his construct. But Westcott and Hort employed the Alexandrian text, not the Textus Receptus which they despised, and the Alexandrian text did not yet exist by AD 68. The Textus Receptus is the original text, and that gives the following construct:

1. [αυτωκαισαρος............¹⁷καιαπο]............18 letters inc. spatium
2. θκριειςοιςειπ]ε[ναυτοιςαποδοτε............28 letters
3. τακαισαρος]**και**[σαρικαιτατου............25 letters
4. θυτωθωκαιε]**θαυ**[μασανεπαυτω............24 letters (stichometry mine)

Even a cursory examination of the 7Q7 fragment shows that the remains of the letter preserved on the top line (Line 2 of our construct) cannot be O (omicron - o), because the base line of the letter is clearly visible, and omicron obviously does not have a base line. Using the stichometry of an average 25 letters to a line allowed by the Textus Receptus whilst employing the traditional *nomina sacra*, however, shows that the letter is E (eta - ε) in its majuscule form, and of course, E in its majuscule form does have a base line.

Line 1 above is merely conjectural, showing how that line would have contained a spatium, or paragraphus, which commonly marked the beginning of a fresh passage or subject in early papyri. The words, of course, are from Textus Receptus as opposed to O'Callaghan's critical text construct. Thiede, for some reason, omitted all reference to 7Q7 in his *Dead Sea Scrolls*, though whether intentionally or accidentally I cannot tell.

But to summarise, in 7Q7 we most certainly have a fragment of Mark 12:17. That much is proven with or without Line 2 of the above construct. Judging by the hooks and flourishes of its letters, the fragment is written in Herodian 'Zierstil,' or 'decorated' style. Although that is the same style of calligraphy in which 7Q5 (Mark 6:52-53) is written, and although the papyrus is of a similar tint and colour, the letters of 7Q7 are written considerably larger (4mm in height) than those of 7Q5, indicating that it is from a separate copy written out by another scribe. That fact, of course, adds considerably to the critics' agony. Multiple copies of any book, signify a library, and in this case, a Christian library! And at Qumran of all places! Whatever next?

Footnotes to Chapter Five

1. O'Callaghan, *Los Papiros Griegos de la Cueva 7 de Qumran.* 1974. p. 69.

2. Ibid.

3. Ibid.

4. Ibid.

5. Ibid., p. 66 – "Escritura grande (altura de las lettras, 4mm.)."

Chapter Six: 7Q8 – James 1:23-24

Fig. 8: 7Q8

7Q8 is one of two fragments from Qumran which make the papyrologist's job pretty straightforward. Like 7Q4.1 (see Chapter One above) whose text runs to the end of each line, making the construction of a stichometry so much easier, so 7Q8 facilitates the fragment's identification by running its text from the beginning of each line. If you can know when a line of text begins or ends, your job is made very much simpler than if the letters were from the middle of a line, for then you have to work in two directions, not just one.

The surviving letters of 7Q8, however, are as follows:

1.   σ[
2.   εσο[
3.   λη[[1]

Allowing a stichometry of exactly 23 letters per line, we are able to identify the fragment as James 1:23-24 thus:

1.   σ[ωποντεσγενεσεωσαυτουεν..........23 letters
2.   εσο[πτρωκατενοησενκαιαπε..........23 letters
3.   λη[λυθενκαιευθεωσεπελαθε..........23 letters[2]

"For if any be a hearer of the word, and not a doer, he is like unto a man beholding his natural face in a glass: For he beholdeth himself, and goeth his way, and straightway forgetteth what manner of man he was." James 1:23-24

There was one concerted, brave, but most definitely unsuccessful attempt by Nebe, Muro, Puech and others to convince everyone that 7Q8, along with other fragments, was actually part of the apocryphal Book of Enoch, and not from James at all. But to make that work, both fragment and Enoch had to be tortured beyond endurance to make them fit together. Thiede answers them all most ably,[3] (see also Chapter Nine below), but the one conclusive proof is the fragment's stichometry. Without any manipulation or stretching whatever – no surmised *spatia*, no estimated *paragraphi*, and definitely no *nomina sacra* - the fragment fits James 1:23-24 like a glove, which it does not do for any other text known to man. It is, in every sense, a perfect fit.

Baillet originally confused matters by adding a tiny fragment detached from some other manuscript which contained the remains of the single letter N (nu = ν), thus artificially creating a fourth line of text.[4] But O'Callaghan was able to show the addition to be erroneous, and for a very good reason. Baillet's additional fragment was written in another hand to that of 7Q8:

"Concerning line 4, my opinion is that N does not belong to the preceding text and is due to another hand."[5] (my translation)

7Q8 is written in the calligraphy favoured by the Herculaneum school, and with that fact emerges an interesting and informative pattern. Wherever the scriptorium was in which the Q7 scrolls were produced, and that was very likely Rome, there were at least four scribes of different schools. Two at least were trained in the 'Zierstil' or decorated style of calligraphy, and the other(s) in the Herculaneum style. This kind of evidence for at least four different scribes shows that the scrolls were issued from the one establishment, and were not an eclectic mix gathered at random over a period of time.

The presence of 7Q8 at Qumran somewhat spoils the critics' persistent claim that James could not have written the letter which goes by his name. The real James, it is pointed out, was put to death in AD 42 by Herod, which is far too early, we are assured, for the writing of this letter. The irony is that the critics rely on the Book of Acts for their information, a book which they have already decried as a forgery. They also forget to notice the fact that James is the only writer of the New Testament to refer to a gathering of Christians as a synagogue. That usage fell out of favour very early on, not surviving the death in AD 44 of the Herod who slew this James. Apart from Jesus Himself, James is the only person in the New Testament to call Hell by the distinctly Jewish name of Gehenna. No other New Testament writer uses that term. So early was he that for James, the only Christians (a term he does not use) were all Jews. No Gentiles had as yet entered the Faith. These, and many other such pointers, indicate a very early date indeed for James' Letter, so it is nothing strange at all for us to find a fragment of a copy of his Letter amongst the other New Testament fragments in Cave 7. No, nothing strange at all.

Robinson provides a most informative discussion of James and his Letter, pointing out, among other things, James' rebuke of rich Jews who defrauded the poor of their wages. There were no rich Jews after AD 70, which is when the critics say this Letter was written, and no poor Jews working their land after that date either - certainly not after the Romans threw out of the land all those whom they did not slaughter. The rebuke would have been meaningless after that year.[6]

Footnotes to Chapter Six

1. O'Callaghan, Los Papiros Griegos de la Cueva 7 de Qumran. 1974. p. 69.

2. O'Callaghan, Los Papiros Griegos de la Cueva 7 de Qumran. 1974. p. 72.

3. Thiede, Dead Sea Scrolls, pp. 163-168.

4. O'Callaghan, Los Papiros Griegos de la Cueva 7 de Qumran. 1974. p. 69.

5. Ibid., p. 70 – "Con respecto la linea 4, mi opinion es que la N no pertenece al texto precedente y se debe a otra mano."

6. Robinson, Redating the New Testament, pp. 118-139.

Chapter Seven: 7Q9 – Romans 5:11-12

Fig. 9: 7Q9

7Q9 is written in the Herodian 'Zierstil' or decorated hand, and its surviving letters are:

1.   ]αγην[
2.   ]Ωσπ[

Constructing a stichometry of 21 and 18 letters respectively to a line, we are able to identify the text of which the fragment is a part, as Romans 5:11-12, thus:

1.   νυντηνκαταλλ]**αγην**[ελαβο.............21 letters
2.   μεν....[12]διατουτο]**ωσπ**[ερδι.............18 letters with spatium[1]

"And not only so, but we also joy in God through our Lord Jesus Christ, by whom we have now received the atonement. Wherefore, as by one man sin entered into the world, and death by sin; and so death passed upon all men, for that all have sinned." Romans 5:11-12

For some reason not explained, O'Callaghan included the word $\varepsilon\nu o\varsigma$ at the end of Line 2 of his stichometry, which would have made the line a little overcrowded with it having to accommodate a spatium, or paragraphus, of 3 or 4 letters.[2] The paragraphus certainly belongs there, for verse 12 carries the reader into a new subject. Omitting $\varepsilon\nu o\varsigma$ from Line 2, and sending it to sit on an imagined Line 3 gives a much tidier stichometry.

Perhaps the greatest point of interest concerning this fragment is not just the presence in the cave of Paul's Letter to the Romans, which he'd written in AD 58 in any case – a full ten years before Qumran Cave 7 was sealed – but the fact that in the cave there was stored a document that has every appearance of being a commentary on Romans (see Chapter Twelve below).[3] It signifies most powerfully how pivotal Paul's Letter to the Romans was – and still is! – to establishing the New Covenant doctrine of salvation through grace by faith. That needed to be clearly explained to the early Church, both Jew and Gentile, and it is interesting to see that commentaries were employed so early on to achieve that end.

Footnotes to Chapter Seven

1. O'Callaghan, *Los Papiros Griegos de la Cueva 7 de Qumran*. 1974. p. 74.

2. Ibid.

3. The fragment of the commentary, which holds several unique features, was catalogued as 7Q19.

Chapter Eight: 7Q10 – 2 Peter 1:15

Fig. 10: 7Q10

This, to my mind, is the most exciting of all the fragments from Cave 7. Its surviving letters are as follows:

1.   ]τ[
2.   ]μηνεξ[¹

....which, given a stichometry of 23 and 21 letters respectively, allows us to identify the fragment as belonging to 2 Peter 1:15:

1.   [δασωδεκαιεκαστο]τ[εεχειν].........23 letters
2.   [υμασμετατηνε]**μηνεξ**[οδον].........21 letters[2]

"Moreover I will endeavour that ye may be able after my decease to have these things always in remembrance." 2 Peter 1:15

The above stichometry is an exact match with the Textus Receptus for 2 Peter 1:15:

"**σπουδασω δε και εκαστοτε εχειν υμας μετα την εμην εξοδον** την τουτων μνημην ποιεισθαι." Stephanus 1550 text (Textus Receptus)

But why is it so exciting to find 2 Peter preserved in Cave 7? For this one glorious reason: 2 Peter is the one Book of the New Testament that critics really do insist is of late composition, written so far beyond the close of the Eyewitness Period, that to even connect it to Peter is ridiculous. It is pseudonymous, nothing more than a pious forgery written years – perhaps a hundred years or more! – after Peter was dead.

With delicious irony, 2 Peter says more in condemnation about false teachers than any other Book of the New Testament, so the critics' insistence on its worthlessness begins to border on the comical.[3] But the added irony is surely the discovery of a fragment of 2 Peter in a cave which was sealed up *within* the Eyewitness Period of AD 30-70; a fragment, moreover, that belonged not to Peter's original Second Letter, but to a copy of it doubtless made from even earlier exemplars, though by how many removes we cannot know. It upends everything that the critics have always taught on the matter. Conservative scholars and Bible apologists have laboured against the critics on this for centuries, but to no avail. Yet the job is done to perfection by a tiny fragment of papyrus which was Providentially preserved in Cave 7. God never – ever! – leaves Himself without a witness. Critics take note.

There is a great deal of evidence for the early writing of 2 Peter besides this fragment, of course - evidence of which the critics are fully aware, but which they always choose to ignore. Occasionally, though, a scholar comes along who sets the record straight.[4]

Footnotes to Chapter Eight

1. O'Callaghan, *Los Papiros Griegos de la Cueva 7 de Qumran.* 1974. p. 75.

2. Ibid.

3. In refreshing contrast to this state of affairs, and for an unusually stout and able defence of Peter's authorship of the letter, see Michael J. Kruger's, "The Authenticity of 2 Peter," *Journal of the Evangelical Theological Society.* Vol. 42.4 (1999). pp. 645-671.

4. Robinson, J. *Redating the New Testament*, pp. 141-199.

Chapter Nine: 7Q11; 7Q12; 7Q13; 7Q14

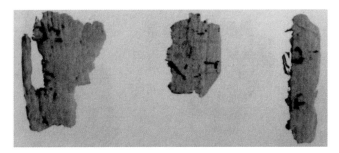

Fig. 11: Fragments 7Q12; 7Q13; 7Q14

Back in the 1980s and 1990s, there was a brave and concerted effort by three leading scholars, Nebe, Muro and Puech, to convince the world that 7Q4, 7Q8 and 7Q12 were actually part and parcel, when combined, of the apocryphal Book of Enoch, instead of being 1 Timothy (7Q4), James (7Q8), and so on.[1] Sadly, the world at large has accepted their proposals uncritically (the irony of it!). But what the world doesn't know is this: the identification is wrong on so many levels that it really shouldn't stand.

Consider. The papyrus of 7Q4 is light brown in colour - "castaño claro" – and is written in Herodian Zierstil script.[2] 7Q8, on the other hand, which is said by Nebe *et collegae* to belong to 7Q4, is somewhat dark brown in colour – "castaño algo oscuro" – and is written out in the Herculaneum style.[3] In contrast, 7Q12, judging by the visual evidence, is written in turn in Herodian Zierstil (see Fig. 11 above). Our three scholars could have saved themselves an enormous amount of time and effort had they taken these simple and observable facts on board before embarking on their attempts to show at all costs that our fragments could not possibly be from the New Testament. The ink that has been spilled in this cause could fill a swimming pool, and all because folks are in such a hurry to disprove a New Testament origin for the Cave 7 fragments, that they fail to see even the simplest facts before them. Pedantry and nit-picking, even when accompanied by scholarly apparati and annotated bibliographies, are all very fine, but if they ignore the primary facts, then they will always and ever come to entirely the wrong conclusion. Each fragment is from a different batch, evidenced by their different colours, and they are written in three different hands under two different styles of calligraphy.

Why was that not noticed at the very beginning? Nebe, Muro and Puech are accomplished scholars, highly regarded in their fields. Yet each of them failed to notice the mismatch in the fragments which would have told them immediately that, whatever these fragments are of, they could never be considered to represent a particularly narrow reference in any single book, never mind the Book of Enoch.

It is remarkable, though, that given the miniscule size of fragments 7Q11; 7Q12; 7Q13; 7Q14, these three scholars still felt themselves able to assert with such confidence that they knew which work they were from, the Book of Enoch, when their first and major objections to the New Testament identification of *any* of the Cave 7 fragments had always rested on the scholarly assertion that in each case the fragments were far too small for any kind of identification to be made. But what is good for the goose, must surely be good for the gander.

Thiede, as always, has done a splendid job of pulling down their assertions by dint of textual analysis, but even he might have saved himself an enormous labour had he spotted the clear differences between these fragments. Using the same critical methodology as Nebe, Muro and Puech, he makes an excellent case for 1 Timothy being the better option, but of course that argument cannot stand if it is built upon the same shifting sands as that of his antagonists. The fact of the matter is, fragments 7Q11; 7Q12; 7Q13; 7Q14, are far too miniscule to be of any use apart from being able to tell us what they are not fragments of.

Footnotes to Chapter Nine

1. Muro, E A. 'The Greek Fragments of Enoch from Qumran Cave 7 (7Q4, 7Q8 & 7Q12 = 7Q en gr = Enoch 103:3-4, 7-8).' *Revue de Qumran.* 70 (1997). pp. 307-311; Nebe, G-W. '7Q4 Möglichkeit und Grenze einer Identifikation.' *Revue de Qumran.* 13 (1988). pp. 629-633; Puech, E. 'Notes sur les fragments grecs du manuscrit 7Q4 = 1 Hénoch 103-105.' *Revue Biblique.* 103 (1996). pp. 592-600; Puech, E. 'Sept fragments grecs de la Lettre d'Hénoch (1 Hén 100, 103 et 105) dans la grotte 7 de Qumran (= 7Q he > ngr).' *Revue de Qumran.* 70 (1997). pp. 313-323.

2. O'Callaghan, *Los Papiros Griegos de la Cueva 7 de Qumran.* 1974. p. 35.

3. Ibid., p. 72.

4. Thiede, *Dead Sea Scrolls*, pp. 163-167.

Chapter Ten: 7Q15 – Mark 6:48

Fig. 12: 7Q15 (*Les Petites Grottes*, Plate XXX)

Different again to all the other Cave 7 fragments is 7Q15. It belongs to the cave's fourth scroll of Mark's Gospel. The papyrus is light brown – "marron claro" – and its script is 'tending to cursive.'[1] The surviving letters are as follows:

1.   ]ντωιελ[
2.   ]σε[ν]α[²

...which, given a stichometry of 22 and 21 letters respectively, allows us to identify them as belonging to Mark 6:48:

1.   [νουσε]**ντωιελ**[αυνεινηνγαρ]...............22 letters
2.   [οανεμο]**σε**[ν]**α**[ντιοσαυτοισ]...............21 letters³

The script has been dated by Roberts to the "First half of the first century A. D."⁴

The text accords exactly with Textus Receptus:

"και ειδεν αυτους βασανιζομε**νους εν τω ελαυνειν ην γαρ ο ανεμος εναντιος αυτοις** και περι τεταρτην φυλακην της νυκτος ερχεται προς αυτους περιπατων επι της θαλασσης και ηθελεν παρελθειν αυτους." Stephanus 1550 (Textus Receptus)

"And He saw them toiling in rowing; for the wind was contrary unto them: and about the fourth watch of the night He cometh unto them, walking upon the sea, and would have passed by them." Mark 6:48

This fragment shows us that we have at least three different scribes writing out copies of Mark's Gospel, the two others writing in Herodian Zierstil and Herculaneum script.

Footnotes to Chapter Ten

1. O'Callaghan, *Los Papiros Griegos de la Cueva 7 de Qumran*. 1974. p. 75-76. – "La escritura de tendencia cursive."

2. Ibid., p. 76.

3. Ibid.

4. Roberts, C. H. *Greek Literary Hands 350 BC – AD 400*. p. 10. cit. also O'Callaghan, *Los Papiros Griegos de la Cueva 7 de Qumran*. 1974. p. 76. n. 2.

Chapter Eleven: 7Q16; 7Q17; 7Q18

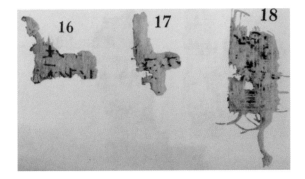

Fig. 13: Fragments 7Q16; 7Q17; 7Q18 (*Les Petites Grottes*, Plate XXX)

The fragments 7Q16; 7Q17; 7Q18 are far too damaged for any meaningful identification to be attempted (see Fig. 13 above). We may assume that they are fragments of New Testament material on the grounds that they were found amongst bigger fragments that most certainly did belong to Books of the New Testament. But apart from that assumption, we may note that 7Q16 appears to have been written in the Herodian Zierstil hand, and perhaps 7Q17 too. But that is all. A great pity.

Chapter Twelve: 7Q19 – A Commentary on Romans?

Fig. 14: 7Q19 (mirror-image of imprint)

7Q19 is one of the most historically intriguing documents we could come across. It is not a fragment of any New Testament Book. But it does appear to be related to the New Testament inasmuch as it seems to be a commentary on one of its Books, and it contains several pointers as to which Book we should be looking at. But 7Q19 is quite unlike the cave's other fragments in another highly unusual way. In fact, in the world of papyrology, it is unique.

Cave 7 at Qumran was excavated between 16th and 19th February 1955. Concerning the state its several fragments were found in, and which features of the cave they were found on, the report mentions some ancient and broken steps inside the cave:

"Most of the written fragments were picked up on these steps. One of the texts, nº 19, was written on papyrus and is preserved only by its imprint on a block of mud. A flake coated with mud likewise bears the imprint of papyrus fibres and the 'stamp' of two Greek letters."[1] (My translation)

Fig. 15: 7Q19 imprint as found

In other words, nothing was left of the papyrus on which the text of 7Q19 had been written. Only its ink remained, imprinted most clearly on what was once a lump of mud. By some exceedingly rare – unique! - process, the ink had somehow transferred itself onto a small wet patch on the floor of the cave, and the papyrus, because it had been made wet, had simply rotted to nothing. But what could have made it wet in such a localised manner? There was no other sign of water damage anywhere in the cave, or on any of the remaining papyrus fragments. Like all the other caves of Qumran, everything was as dry as a bone. But there is perhaps a clue.

The forensic analysis of the Cave 7 fragments conducted by the Israel National Police Laboratory in Jerusalem (see Appendix below) mentions the clear evidence of violence that the fragments had suffered.[2] 7Q5 particularly showed signs of this, exhibiting both a hole and a tear in its fabric. The jar in which the scrolls had been stored had been smashed and its pieces scattered all over the cave floor, and the papyrus fragments had mostly been retrieved scattered over the steps inside the cave. Someone, a Roman soldier no doubt, had clearly ripped up the scrolls and carried their remains away from the jar and over the steps to dump the bulk of the remains outside the cave, perhaps to show them to an officer, where they perished. But by his carrying them outside, several scraps had fallen to the floor and also upon the steps where they were to lay undisturbed for the next 1,887 years.

The person who did all this was most probably a soldier of the Tenth Legion which was, in AD 68, hunting down any Jewish rebels that they could find at Qumran as well as anywhere else in Judaea. We know from finds in other caves at Qumran that the Romans had broken into some of the caves, hoping to find fugitives in there, and finding none, vandalised their contents. Here it seems that one of them, whilst vandalising the contents of Cave 7, had shown his contempt for these Jewish books by urinating on one of them. What more natural and expected? Like others before and since, Roman soldiers in the field in time of war were never noted for their mastery of potty training. But this act of contempt was to Providentially preserve the words of 7Q19 in a unique and unheard-of way, and allow us to see the contents of Cave 7 in a wholly unexpected light.

What we appear to be looking at in 7Q19 – the largest fragment of text found in Cave 7 by the way – is a commentary on Paul's Letter to the Romans. How can we possibly know that from such a small fragment? Here's how:

7Q19 bears 34 letters on six lines of text. They do not match any New Testament text, nor any extant non-Biblical Greek text. But they are as follows:

1.   ]η[
2.   ]ηλχ(?)[
3.   ]χταιαπο[
4.   ...]ησχτισεω[
5.   ]ενταισγραφα[
6.   ....]οαν[³

It's pointless offering any stichometry on the fragment, for there is no known text against which to test it. But these surviving letters make up words, and it is the words – words that are uniquely put and which make sense - that betray the text of which this scroll was once a commentary. Let's see how that works.

Thiede provides a four-page technical appraisal of the text,[4] but the basic facts are these. In lines 4 and 5 of the fragment, we have words that refer to the Creation – τ]ης κτισεω[ς – in direct reference to the Scriptures – εν ταις γραφα[ις – which together combine to tell us both the nature of the text, and even which Book of the New Testament is being referred to here. It was enough to frighten the editors of the *editio princeps*, Baillet and colleagues, for they tried to throw a most non-committal pall over the subject.[5] But the evidence is clear and powerful, not least for the fact that outside Paul's Letter to the Romans, the words are unique:

"...[the] text as we have it on 7Q19 cannot be traced in the Greek Bible [i.e. the LXX], nor in any other known apocryphal text, nor in Greek literature as a whole."[6]

Now here is where it gets interesting. Thiede points out that it was the invariable habit of Jewish Greek writers and commentators on the Greek version of the Old Testament (LXX) to always place the epithet 'holy' ('ιερος) before the word 'Scriptures.'[7] Even Josephus, writing long after, conforms to this habit. Yet for some reason unknown to us, our New Testament writers did not conform to this habit. Instead, they simply refer to the Scriptures. The only exception is the one occasion when Paul, writing in Romans (1:2), speaks of the holy Scriptures, but then he places the epithet for 'holy' ('αγιαις) *behind* the word for Scriptures (εν γραφαις αγιαις).[8]

Now we see the same usage, namely the omission of the epithet 'holy' before the word for Scriptures, in Line 5 of our fragment, 7Q19 – εν ταις γραφα[ις – 'in the Scriptures.' We cannot know if Paul's 'αγιαις – 'holy' – followed the word γραφαις on the fragment, but we do know that the omission of the conventional 'ιερος marks this out as a document pertaining to the New Testament by a writer who conformed to the newly-adopted New Testament convention of always omitting the 'ιερος epithet. Moreover, whether he copied Paul by adding 'αγιαις afterward or not, does not spoil the identification. 7Q19 is a document that pertains to and concerns the New Testament. But how do we know that it concerns in particular Paul's Letter to the Romans? Because in Romans 8:19, Paul speaks of the Creation – "της κτισεως" – in the same genitive clause as we find in 7Q19.[9]

Now the ramifications of this are immense – truly immense. We know from the presence of fragment 7Q9 in Cave 7 that Paul's Letter to the Romans (which was some ten years old by AD 68) was known and used by whoever placed the New Testament scrolls in the cave. And by the presence and nature of 7Q19 in that cave, we know that Paul's Romans was not only read, but studied, and studied in depth. Concerning which, there is an interesting remark by Peter in which he says:

"As also in all his [Paul's] epistles, speaking in them of these things; in which are some things hard to be understood, which they that are unlearned and unstable wrest, as they do also the other Scriptures, unto their own destruction." 2 Peter 3:16

Interestingly, just three verses before, Peter had been talking of the new Creation before referring to Paul and urging believers to read Paul's letters, some of which, he had to confess, contained things that were hard to understand. Notice also how Peter follows the New Testament convention of omitting the epithet 'holy' before 'Scriptures' and even after. Earlier in his third chapter, in the 4th verse to be precise, Peter even uses the same word for the old Creation (κτισεως) in its genitive case as both Paul and 7Q19 use.

Now when Peter mentioned the difficulty of some of Paul's letters, he was saying nothing that his readers did not also feel, and it would seem by the writing of this commentary on Romans that someone took his words very seriously and attempted to supply the need. Critics, of course, have trouble accepting that *any* of the New Testament Books had been written by AD 68, so they now have to explain how it comes about that commentaries existed on those Books even before that date. No man can offer comments on books which have not yet been written, so even if 7Q19 had been the only fragment found in Cave 7, we would know by its existence that at least one New Testament Book, namely Romans, had been written and put into circulation beforehand.

Now if the fragments of Cave 7 (7Q4.1-7Q19) had been exclusively of Books of the New Testament, then they could be called a collection. But the presence of this commentary turns that collection into a library, a reference library no less in which books are not just read, but studied as well. This is very much enforced when we consider the multiple copies of Mark's Gospel, at least four copies of which that were found together, written by four different scribes in three distinct styles of calligraphy. That speaks powerfully of a production centre, a professional scriptorium no less, meaning at the very least that some scholars have a great deal of rewriting to do, especially those who would have us believe that the Gospels especially were born of 'oral tradition' passed down through three or four generations before someone had the bright idea of writing them down. Will that happen? No, I don't suppose it will. But at least now Bible believers can rest assured that their New Testament is indeed an eyewitness account, and no collection of fables.

Footnotes to Chapter Twelve

1. Baillet M, Milik J, & Vaux R (eds.). 'Les Petites Grottes de Qumran.' *Discoveries in the Judaean Desert*. Vol. 3. pp. 27-28. - "La plupart des fragments écrits ont été remassés sur ces marches. Un des textes, n° 19, était écrit sur papyrus et ne conservé que par son décalque sur un bloc de boue. Un tesson couvert de boue porte également l'empreinte de fibres de papyrus et le décalque de deux lettres grecques."

2. Thiede, 'Bericht über die kriminaltechnische Untersuchung des Fragments 7Q5 in Jerusalem.' *Christen und Christliche*. pp. 239-245. – "The theory put forward for Cave 4 that the Romans, in AD 68 or shortly thereafter, discovered and smashed the jar and ripped up the scrolls inside, explaining the 800 small fragments in that cave, applies as well to Cave 7. The solitary jar that was found smashed, along with a few scraps of papyrus, show that 7Q5 at least, (and perhaps the two pieces of 7Q4), with their traces of wanton destruction, fit into this scenario." (my translation)

3. Thiede, *Rekindling the Word*, p. 200.

4. Thiede, *The Dead Sea Scrolls*, pp. 142-145.

5. Baillet M, Milik J, & Vaux R (eds.). 'Les Petites Grottes de Qumran.' *Discoveries in the Judaean Desert*. Vol. 3. pp. 145-146. - "Les quelques mots que l'on peut saisir font penser à un texte de caractère théologique." – "The few words that one can capture make one think of a text of a theological nature." (my translation)

6. Thiede, *The Dead Sea Scrolls*, p. 143.

7. Thiede, 'Das unbeachtete Qumran-Fragment 7Q19 und die Herkunft der Höhle 7.' *Aegyptus*. 74 (1994). pp. 123-128. Also, Thiede, *Dead Sea Scrolls*, pp. 143-145.

8. "ο προεπηγγειλατο δια των προφητων αυτου εν γραφαις αγιαις." Romans 1:2.

9. Thiede, *The Dead Sea Scrolls*, p. 145.

Chapter Thirteen: What Happened to Cave 7?

Fig. 16: Cave 7 Destroyed

Yes, what did happen to Cave 7? As can be seen in Fig. 16 above, there is now a gaping great hole where Cave 7 once stood. How is it that the cave has now utterly disappeared, roof, walls and all? It is a mystery - or maybe not.

On 20th October 1991, a symposium at the Catholic University of Eichstätt in Germany wrote to Mr Drori, Director of the Department of Antiquities at Jerusalem, asking that Cave 7 at Qumran be re-excavated by a qualified and approved archaeological team:

"...we, the undersigned, established the need for a renewed investigation of the area of this cave which has since collapsed into the Wadi Qumran."[1]

Exactly why, how and when it collapsed is not mentioned in the letter, which is undersigned by sixteen members of the symposium, (Thiede's name and signature appear last of all on the list), though the context very much suggests a recent event.. The members went on to ask that the Israeli Department of Antiquities itself assign their own archaeologists to the task (at the university's expense), which elicited, on 12th November 1991, the following response from Dr Yitzhak Magen, Archaeological Staff Officer for Judea and Samaria:

"....the cave you mention is situated in the locality for which I am responsible. We are planning, in the near future, to begin a large-scale excavation in the Judean desert and Qumran areas and will then re-examine again (sic) Cave 7."[2]

It's the "re-examine again" which bothers me. Are we to assume from this that it had already been 're-examined'? If so, when, and by whom? What did they find, and what has become of their report? None has been published, certainly, and it would seem by the thunderous silence that has since pervaded the subject, that Cave 7 – or rather the nothing that's left of it - is still waiting to be 're-examined again.'

But it still doesn't explain how a sizeable and substantially housed cave has just disappeared like this. Yes, it collapsed, the story goes, at some unrecorded moment between 1972 and 1991 (most likely in the late 1980s), and fell into the Wadi Qumran below. But caves that have stood for some 1900 years or more do not simply collapse without a reason. So might it have been erosion?

Erosion by what? Qumran has to be one of the driest and most tranquil places on earth. Windless too. Witness how those scraps of papyrus lay on the steps in the entrance to the cave for a full 1,887 years without disturbance. In any ordinary location, they wouldn't have lain there a day. You can still see the remains of the steps that led up into the cave in Fig. 16 above. They were not that far inside when the cave still stood. Yet still the scraps of papyrus were able to lie on them undisturbed for all those years – for all those centuries. So again we ask, what caused the cave to collapse?

It is a matter of historical record that O'Callaghan's 1972 announcement to the world that the cave contained New Testament documents caused an unholy furore. A great many people were deeply angered by it – they still are! - and so too were a great many powerful institutions – anti-Christian institutions around the world who have worked for decades to bring down the New Testament and discredit it utterly in the public's eyes. There were lively fears and suspicions among them that the cave could yield yet more evidence for the pre-AD 68 antiquity of the New Testament, hopeful expectations that were still being voiced by the Eichstätt Symposium as late as 1991 even after the cave was no more. So again we ask, what, or who, was responsible for the cave's destruction?

Famous though it is, Qumran and its desert environs remain unvisited by humans for much of the year, which is why illicit diggers are able to so freely excavate and smuggle away antiquities from the area in spite of the watchful eye of the Israeli Antiquities Authority. The members of the Eichstätt Symposium voiced their own fears in their letter to Drori of illicit excavations spoiling the archaeology of Qumran:

"Furthermore, such an investigation would appear to be urgent in view of the vigorous attempts of amateur diggers to start their own campaigns at or near Caves 3, 7, and so forth."[3]

In short, if anyone had wished to destroy the cave because of what it represented, and to forestall any further excavations and finds of New Testament Books and documents there, then they would not have lacked either the opportunity or the privacy in which to demolish the cave unseen. The timing and manner of the cave's disappearance is simply too suspicious to allow any theory of a natural catastrophe having occurred. There is simply no sign of that. All there is to see is the gaping great hole where Cave 7 so recently stood. Re-examine again? There's nothing to re-examine. Had any fragments still remained in that cave, they would have been pulverised to destruction in the fall of the cave's roof and walls as they fell in on top of them.

But then that only raises the following question: Was nature ever so tidy as this? Had the cave simply collapsed under its own weight, or by some other natural means, then where are the many tons of debris that should now be lying on the shelf that was once the cave's floor? – the remains of the substantial roof and walls whose fall would, if having occurred naturally, have been arrested by the floor of the cave? Where are they? The shelf is empty. The shelf is swept clean.

I firmly believe that we are looking here, not at the hand of nature, but at the hand of man for the cave's destruction. Of the two, only man destroys evidence and then cleans up behind him. Someone has cleared the site and swept it clean of demolition rubble, seeking to obliterate all traces of the cave and prevent any further discoveries there. Whoever did it, or even when they did it during the nineteen years that passed between 1972 and 1991, is unknown to us, and so it will remain no doubt. But whoever it was, and whenever they did the deed, they wasted their time.

The New Testament fragments from Qumran were identified and published by O'Callaghan in 1972; were again publicised and most ably defended by Thiede in the 1990s; and are here being published once again for all the world to see. They are safely housed and preserved in the Rockefeller Museum at Jerusalem, and they are not going to go away.

Nor should they. The cave may have gone, but the fragments remain. They stand as immensely trustworthy witnesses to the one single fact that is hated today amongst the critics and unbelievers – that the New Testament was written out, copied and disseminated over parts of the Roman Empire during the forty-year Eyewitness Period (AD 30-70) by people who would have seen and heard our Lord speak, perform miracles, give His Life on the cross, and then rise from the dead. They bear glorious testimony to the fact that the Gospels did not begin as orally transmitted tales that were eventually written down years after the Eyewitness Period was closed. They are contemporary records written down by people who saw and heard the things that they wrote about, and not idle tales half recalled by old men as they entertained their grandchildren. That is the value of the Qumran Cave 7 fragments, and that is why they are hated – hated enough, it seems, for someone to demolish even the very cave that they were found in. But they cannot demolish the evidence of the Q7 fragments. That at least remains, and remains for all time to bear witness to the antiquity and authenticity of the New Testament, and to the Truth of the Word of God.

Footnotes to Chapter Thirteen

1. *Christen und Christliches in Qumran?*, pp. 247-248 (here unpaginated for some reason).

2. Ibid., p. 249 (again unpaginated).

3. Ibid., p. 247 (unpaginated).

Chapter Fourteen: Conclusion

Why should Rome be looked to for the provenance of the scrolls that were once stored in Q7? There are many reasons. Firstly, there are the scribal habits and styles of calligraphy that are seen on the fragments. These are typically Roman. There are the remains of the jar in which the Q7 scrolls had been stored, the shoulder of which still bears twice the name of Rome in Hebrew characters (אמור). But beyond even these evidences, there is the immediate and recognisable impact that Mark's Gospel – the only Gospel that was found in Q7 – had upon the people, the society, and the literati of Rome. We have Petronius, during the reign of Nero, writing his boisterous novel, *The Feast of Trimalchio*, in which he openly mocks Mark 14:3-9 & 17-72. In his earlier *Satyrica* (141), he satirises Mark 14:22. Then there's Chariton, writing even earlier during the reign of either Caligula or Claudius, his novel *Chaireas and Callirhoe* (3:3), in which he openly pillories Mark's account of the our Lord's empty tomb and His Resurrection.[1] One simply should not ignore such evidences as these, but ignored they are in almost every paper, commentary, dictionary and book about the Bible.

Ignored again is the relevance – the immense ramifications – of the Q7 fragments, and the colossal impact that they could have on modern Bible scholarship, if only the world of scholarship would let them be heard. Not that that will ever happen. There are far too many careers at stake, not to mention centuries of hard work dedicated to the downgrading and ultimate destruction of the Scriptures. But they are published here for the edification and encouragement of all those millions who love the Bible, and who delight to see it vindicated.

Footnote to Chapter Fourteen

1. For a detailed account, see Cooper, *The Authenticity of the New Testament Part 1: The Gospels* - Chapter Six: The Authenticity of Mark's Gospel.

Appendix One: Report on the forensic examination of the fragment 7Q5 in Jerusalem

Translated out of Thiede's 'Bericht über die kriminaltechnische Untersuchung des Fragments 7Q5 in Jerusalem.' *Christen und Christliche.* pp. 239-245.

On Sunday, 12th April 1992 ([Sunday is] a working day in Israel), the Qumran fragment 7Q5 was examined by forensic technology at the Israel National Police Investigations Department (Division of Identification and Forensic Science). The committee governing the Israel Antiquities Authority had granted approval for transporting the glass plate with the 7Q fragments. Curator Joseph Zia conducted the transfer of the fragments from the John Rockefeller Museum to the Police Laboratory in the Sheikh Jarrah Neighbourhood. Brigadier General Dr Joseph Almog, Director of the Department, was responsible for the work by the Division of Identification and Forensic Science. The examination for this report was carried out by Chief Inspector Sharon Landau in the presence of the aforementioned gentlemen and the author.[1] The key stages of the examination were recorded by a television crew from Bayerischen Rundfunks [a Bavarian television company].[2]

The aim of the study was to answer two questions in the short time available:

1. Is the fragment 7Q5 in an unfalsified condition without recent (human) tampering or changes?

2. Can it be determined that the remains of the letter in the middle of Line 2, generally considered to be crucial for identification, are two adscript letters, e.g. *Iota* follows *Alpha*? Or is it one letter, namely a *Nu*?

At Eichstätt,[3] several specimens of *Nu*s were presented by Herbert Hunger, the Viennese papyrologist, which showed considerable variations [of the letter *Nu*] within a single manuscript written by a single scribe. This is clearly seen between the complete *Nu* of Line 4 and the reconstructed *Nu* of Line 2 of the 7Q5 fragment. Hunger went on to say that *Nu* is not just a possibility in Line 2, but may be confidently asserted to be *Nu*.[4]

The forensic examination showed that Question 1 has a quick and clear answer: it is absolutely certain that no subsequent alterations have been made to the text of 7Q5. The visible stock of the letter matches the original visible remains. It must remain open whether the severe damage, especially to the right side of the fragment (a turn to the right above the tear), be attributed to early human interference. The theory put forward for Cave 4 that the Romans, in AD 68 or shortly thereafter, discovered and smashed the jar and ripped up the scrolls inside, explaining the 800 small fragments in that cave, applies as well to Cave 7. The solitary jar that was found smashed, along with a few scraps of papyrus, show that 7Q5 at least, (and perhaps the two pieces of 7Q4), with their traces of wanton destruction, fit into this scenario.

The stereo-microscope examination of Line 2 of 7Q5 which followed, showed the clearly discernible remnants of a stroke running diagonally from top left to bottom right, beginning at the top of that vertical line which is either an *Iota adscript*[5] or the left vertical line of a [letter] *Nu*. Owing to the discovery of that diagonal line, the possibility of it being an *Iota* is finally excluded. Although the full length of the visible line is not preserved entirely, it is long enough to exclude the possibility of it being a *Rho*. It is clearly the diagonal line of a *Nu*, as would be required for the identification of 7Q5 as Mark 6:52-53.

This is an important step toward confirming the identification. The *Nu* in Line 2 is now one of the 'dependable characters' of the fragment, and it is evidence, for critics and proponents alike, that is in favour of the identification of Mark. Moreover, it confirms O'Callaghan's readings with the aid of the Ibycus Computer programme. And the investigation carried out at Liverpool yielded only Mark 6:52-53 for 7Q5.

Nonetheless, questions do remain. As well as identifying the Line 2 character as a *Nu*, the forensic examination also confirmed Herbert Hunger's thesis concerning the wide differences that can occur between the same letters within the same fragment. For instance, the two undoubted *Eta*s of [7Q5], make possible the identification of the remnants of another *Eta* to the right of the tear on Line 2.

The Jerusalem laboratory, however, was unable to make certain ink remains visible even where they once undoubtedly existed. For example, the vertical stroke of the *Kappa* of Line 3; in the conjunction of *Alpha* and *Iota* of the *kai* in Line 3; or even the vertical stroke of the *Nu* of Line 2.

In some places, the ink has disappeared altogether while it is still visible in others, depending on how deep both ink and pen penetrated the papyrus. The diagonal stroke of the *Nu* of Line 2 shows how the scribe pressed hard at top left, so that the ink can still be seen under extreme magnification.

The examination of the [7Q] fragments is ongoing. The investigation of 7Q5 will continue under much improved instrumentation, and this applies to the other fragments as well. The fact that the forensic examination of 7Q5 has yielded such firm results, has encouraged all parties toward this end.

Footnotes to Appendix One

1. Dr Carsten Peter Thiede.

2. "The forensic analysis of 7Q5 and its recording by Bavarian Television was part of the documentary *'Der unbekannte Jesus'* (The unknown Jesus) which was shown on the first Channel (ARD) on 7.6.1992 in a sixty minute version, as well as in two forty-five minute programmes on 20.8.92 (repeat 23.8.92) and on 27.8.92 (repeat 30.8.92) on the Third Channel of Bavarian Television as well as on 1.9 and 6.9.1992 on Eins Plus." *Rekindling the Word*, p. 197.

3. The Eichstätt Symposium papers are published in *Christen und Christliches in Qumran?*. 1992. Friedrich Pustet.

4. Hunger, H. '7Q5: Markus 6:52-53 – oder? Die Meinung des Papyrologen.' *Christen und Christliches in Qumran?*. 1992. Friedrich Pustet. pp. 33-56.

5. An 'Iota adscript' is the joining together (in this case) of the letters alpha α and iota ι, as in the word *kai*, partial remnants of which might give the impression of a nu v when written in majuscule.

Bibliography

Baillet M, Milik J, & Vaux R (eds.). 'Les Petites Grottes de Qumran.' *Discoveries in the Judaean Desert.* Vol. 3. (issued in 2 vols: *Textes et Planches*). 1962. Clarendon Press, Oxford.

Estrada, D & White, W. *The First New Testament.* 1978. Thomas Nelson. New York.

Kruger, Michael J. 'The Authenticity of 2 Peter.' *Journal of the Evangelical Theological Society.* Vol. 42.4 (1999). pp. 645-671.

Liddell, H G & Scott R. *A Greek-English Lexicon.* 1882. New York.

Muro, E A. 'The Greek Fragments of Enoch from Qumran Cave 7 (7Q4, 7Q8 & 7Q12 = 7Q en gr = Enoch 103:3-4, 7-8).' *Revue de Qumran.* 70 (1997). pp. 307-311.

Nebe, G-W. '7Q4 Möglichkeit und Grenze einer Identifikation.' *Revue de Qumran.* 13 (1988). pp. 629-633.

O'Callaghan, José. 'Papiros neotestamentarios en la cueva 7 de Qumran?' *Biblica.* 53 (1972). pp. 91-100. – This was translated into English by Holliday: 'New Testament Papyri in Qumran Cave 7?' *Journal of Biblical Literature.* 91 (1972). Supplement, pp. 1-14. The supplement also contains an English translation from the Italian of Carlo Martini's, 'Note sui papyri della grotto 7 di Qumran.' *Biblica.* 53 (1972). pp. 101-104.

O'Callaghan, José. 'Notas sobre 7Q tomadas en el Rockefeller Museum de Jerusalén.' *Biblica.* 53 (1972), pp. 517-533. (Tabulae extra seriem).

O'Callaghan, José. 'Tres probables papiros neotestimentarios en la cueva 7 de Qumran.' *Studia Papyrologica.* 11 (1972). pp. 83-89.

O'Callaghan, José. 'El cambio δ>τ-en los papiros biblicos.' *Biblica.* 54 (1973), pp. 415-416.

O'Callaghan, José. 'Les papyrus de la grotte 7 de Qumran.' *Nouvelle Revue Theologique.* 95 (1973), pp. 187-195.

O'Callaghan, José. 'La identificacion de papiros literarios (biblicos).' *Studia Papyrologica.* 12 (1973), pp. 91-100.

O'Callaghan, José. 'El ordenador, 7Q5 y Homero.' *Studia Papyrologica.* 12 (1973), pp. 73-79.

O'Callaghan, José. *Los Papiros Griegos de la Cueva 7 de Qumran.* 1974. Biblioteca de Autores Cristianos. Madrid.

O'Callaghan, José. 'El ordenador, 7Q5 y los autores griegos (Apolonio de Rodas, Aristoteles, Lisias).' *Studia Papyrologica.* 13 (1974), pp. 21-29.

O'Callaghan, José. 'Notas sobre 7Q4 y 7Q5.' *Studia Papyrologica.* 13 (1974), pp. 61-63.

O'Callaghan, José. 'El texto de 7Q5 es Tuc. I 41,2?' *Studia Papyrologica*. 13 (1974), p. 125.

O'Callaghan, José. 'The Identifications of 7Q.' *Aegyptus*. Anno 56, No, 1-4. (Gennaio-Decembre 1976). pp. 287-294.

O'Callaghan, José. '7Q5: Nuevas consideraciones.' *Studia Papyrologica*. 16 (1977), pp. 41-47.

O'Callaghan, José. 'El cambio δ>τ en P. Chester Beatty XIII.' *Biblica*. 60 (1979), pp. 567-569.

O'Callaghan, José. 'La Biblia y los papiros.' *Unidad y pluralidaden el Mundo Antiguo*. Actas des VI Congresso Espanol de Estudos Clasicos, I Ponencias (Sevilla, 6-11 de abril de 1981). 1983. Madrid. pp. 413-434.

O'Callaghan, José. 'Verso le origini del Nuevo Testamento.' *La Civilta Cattolica*. 4 (1988), pp. 269-272.

O'Callaghan, José. 'Papyri Manuscripts of the Gospels.' *The Gospels Today: A Guide to Some Recent Developments*. 1990. Philadelphia. pp. 503-510.

Puech, E. 'Notes sur les fragments grecs du manuscrit 7Q4 = 1 Hénoch 103-105.' *Revue Biblique*. 103 (1996). pp. 592-600.

Puech, E. 'Sept fragments grecs de la Lettre d'Hénoch (1 Hén 100, 103 et 105) dans la grotte 7 de Qumran (= 7Q he > ngr).' *Revue de Qumran*. 70 (1997). pp. 313-323.

Roberts, C H. *Greek Literary Hands* 350 BC – AD 400. 1955. Clarendon Press. Oxford.

Robinson, J. *Redating the New Testament*. 1976. SCM Press. London.

Smith, D & Tyson J (eds.). *Acts and Christian Beginnings: The Acts Seminar Report*. 2013. Polebridge Press. (Westar Institute).

Thiede, Carsten Peter. *The Earliest Gospel Manuscript?* 1992. Paternoster Press.

Thiede, Carsten Peter. 'Bericht über die kriminaltechnische Untersuchung des Fragments 7Q5 in Jerusalem.' *Christen und Christliches in Qumran?*. 1992. Friedrich Pustet. pp. 239-245.

Thiede, Carsten Peter. 'Greek Qumran Fragment 7Q5: Possibilities and Impossibilities.' *Biblica*. Vol. 75. No. 3 (1994), pp. 394-398.

Thiede, Carsten Peter. *Rekindling the Word: In Search of Gospel Truth*. 1995. Gracewing.

Thiede, Carsten Peter. *The Dead Sea Scrolls and the Jewish Origins of Christianity*. 2000. Lion Publishing. Oxford.

AN ALADDIN'S CAVE OF FOSSILS AND GEMS...
IN A JUNGLE ATMOSPHERE WHERE A 7 METRE DINOSAUR MODEL LURKS...

FREE ENTRY

DISCOVER

GENESIS EXPO

NEWLY EXPANDED!

www.csm.org.uk

**TUESDAY to SATURDAY 11AM - 4PM AND BANK HOLIDAYS
(CLOSED CHRISTMAS TO NEW YEAR)**

17 - 18 THE HARD, PORTSMOUTH (100M FROM DOCKYARD GATE)

IN THIS TIME OF INCREDIBLE SCIENTIFIC ADVANCE, WHEN WE CAN SEE THE FAR UNIVERSE, COMMUNICATE WORLDWIDE AND CURE DISEASES, MANY PEOPLE STILL CHOOSE TO BELIEVE THAT LIVING THINGS ALL HAPPENED BY CHANCE. THE GENESIS EXPO SETS OUT TO DEMONSTRATE THAT THE UNIVERSE, AND EVERYTHING IN IT, WAS DESIGNED. LET YOUR ADVENTURE BEGIN...

Further publications by Bill Cooper available from CSM

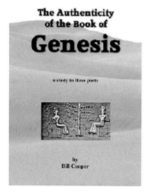

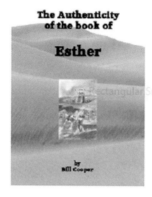

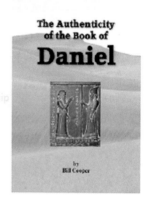

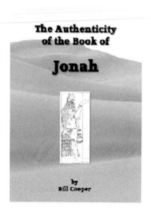

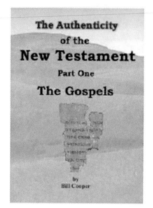

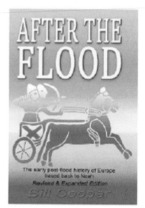

Creation Science Movement

PO Box 888, Portsmouth PO6 2YD, UK
Facebook: Creation-Science-Movement/
www.csm.org.uk; info@csm.org.uk; 02392 293988

Buy At
www.genesisexpo.org.uk/shop

Further publications by Bill Cooper available from CSM

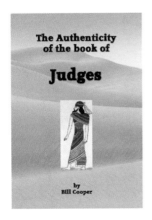

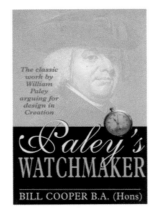

More Books
by
Bill Cooper
coming
soon!

Visit the 'Bill Cooper' website at

www.billcooper.org.uk
www.authenticity.billcooper.org.uk

Buy At
www.genesisexpo.org.uk/shop